Adding 1

1+1 to 9+1

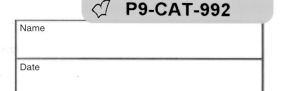

P9-CAT-992

Name

Date

To parents
Understanding the concept of adding 1 is a basic step in learning addition. When your child completes each exercise, please offer lots of praise. Some pages contain a number chart to give children a hint that the answers are included in the chart.

■ Add the numbers below.

(1) 1 + 1 =

(2) 2 + 1 =

(3) 3 + 1 =

(4) 4 + 1 =

(5) 5 + 1 =

(6) 6 + 1 =

(7) 7 + 1 =

(8) 8 + 1 =

(9) 9 + 1 =

(10) 1 + 1 =

(11) 2 + 1 =

(12) 3 + 1 =

(13) 5 + 1 =

(14) 4 + 1 =

(15) 6 + 1 =

(16) 8 + 1 =

(17) 9 + 1 =

(18) 7 + 1 =

(19) 8 + 1 =

(20) 9 + 1 =

| 1 | 2 | 3 | 4 | 5 | 6 | 7 | 8 | 9 | 10 |

10+1 to 19+1

■ Add the numbers below.

(1) $10 + 1 =$

(2) $11 + 1 =$

(3) $12 + 1 =$

(4) $13 + 1 =$

(5) $14 + 1 =$

(6) $15 + 1 =$

(7) $16 + 1 =$

(8) $17 + 1 =$

(9) $18 + 1 =$

(10) $19 + 1 =$

(11) $12 + 1 =$

(12) $15 + 1 =$

(13) $10 + 1 =$

(14) $13 + 1 =$

(15) $11 + 1 =$

(16) $14 + 1 =$

(17) $17 + 1 =$

(18) $18 + 1 =$

(19) $16 + 1 =$

(20) $19 + 1 =$

11	12	13	14	15	16	17	18	19	20

Name

Date

■ Add the numbers below.

(1) $20 + 1 =$

(2) $21 + 1 =$

(3) $22 + 1 =$

(4) $23 + 1 =$

(5) $24 + 1 =$

(6) $25 + 1 =$

(7) $26 + 1 =$

(8) $27 + 1 =$

(9) $28 + 1 =$

(10) $29 + 1 =$

(11) $26 + 1 =$

(12) $23 + 1 =$

(13) $29 + 1 =$

(14) $20 + 1 =$

(15) $27 + 1 =$

(16) $22 + 1 =$

(17) $24 + 1 =$

(18) $21 + 1 =$

(19) $25 + 1 =$

(20) $28 + 1 =$

| 21 | 22 | 23 | 24 | 25 | 26 | 27 | 28 | 29 | 30 |

■ Add the numbers below.

(1)   1 + 1 =

(2)   2 + 1 =

(3)   4 + 1 =

(4)   6 + 1 =

(5)   7 + 1 =

(6)   8 + 1 =

(7)   11 + 1 =

(8)   12 + 1 =

(9)   15 + 1 =

(10)   16 + 1 =

(11)   17 + 1 =

(12)   18 + 1 =

(13)   19 + 1 =

(14)   21 + 1 =

(15)   22 + 1 =

(16)   24 + 1 =

(17)   25 + 1 =

(18)   26 + 1 =

(19)   27 + 1 =

(20)   29 + 1 =

3 Adding 2
1+2 to 8+2

Name

Date

To parents
Starting with this page, your child will practice addition formulas that include the number 2. If your child is having difficulty with adding 2, please encourage him or her to return to practice that includes adding 1 before proceeding.

■ Add the numbers below.

(1) $1 + 2 =$

(2) $2 + 2 =$

(3) $3 + 2 =$

(4) $4 + 2 =$

(5) $5 + 2 =$

(6) $6 + 2 =$

(7) $7 + 2 =$

(8) $8 + 2 =$

(9) $4 + 2 =$

(10) $5 + 2 =$

(11) $1 + 2 =$

(12) $3 + 2 =$

(13) $2 + 2 =$

(14) $6 + 2 =$

(15) $8 + 2 =$

(16) $7 + 2 =$

(17) $5 + 2 =$

(18) $8 + 2 =$

(19) $6 + 2 =$

(20) $7 + 2 =$

| 1 | 2 | 3 | 4 | 5 | 6 | 7 | 8 | 9 | 10 |

9+2 to 18+2

■ Add the numbers below.

(1) $9 + 2 =$

(2) $10 + 2 =$

(3) $11 + 2 =$

(4) $12 + 2 =$

(5) $13 + 2 =$

(6) $14 + 2 =$

(7) $15 + 2 =$

(8) $16 + 2 =$

(9) $17 + 2 =$

(10) $18 + 2 =$

(11) $14 + 2 =$

(12) $12 + 2 =$

(13) $10 + 2 =$

(14) $13 + 2 =$

(15) $9 + 2 =$

(16) $15 + 2 =$

(17) $11 + 2 =$

(18) $18 + 2 =$

(19) $16 + 2 =$

(20) $17 + 2 =$

| 11 | 12 | 13 | 14 | 15 | 16 | 17 | 18 | 19 | 20 |

4 **Adding 2**
19+2 to 28+2

Name

Date

■ Add the numbers below.

(1) $19 + 2 =$

(2) $20 + 2 =$

(3) $21 + 2 =$

(4) $22 + 2 =$

(5) $23 + 2 =$

(6) $24 + 2 =$

(7) $25 + 2 =$

(8) $26 + 2 =$

(9) $27 + 2 =$

(10) $28 + 2 =$

(11) $19 + 2 =$

(12) $21 + 2 =$

(13) $23 + 2 =$

(14) $24 + 2 =$

(15) $20 + 2 =$

(16) $22 + 2 =$

(17) $27 + 2 =$

(18) $28 + 2 =$

(19) $25 + 2 =$

(20) $26 + 2 =$

| 21 | 22 | 23 | 24 | 25 | 26 | 27 | 28 | 29 | 30 |

1+2 to 28+2

■ Add the numbers below.

(1)   1 + 2 =

(2)   2 + 2 =

(3)   3 + 2 =

(4)   6 + 2 =

(5)   7 + 2 =

(6)   8 + 2 =

(7)   9 + 2 =

(8)   11 + 2 =

(9)   12 + 2 =

(10) 13 + 2 =

(11) 16 + 2 =

(12) 17 + 2 =

(13) 19 + 2 =

(14) 21 + 2 =

(15) 22 + 2 =

(16) 23 + 2 =

(17) 25 + 2 =

(18) 26 + 2 =

(19) 27 + 2 =

(20) 28 + 2 =

5 Review
Adding 1 and 2

Name

Date

To parents
Starting with this page, your child will review addition that includes the numbers 1 and 2. If he or she is having difficulty solving addition that includes adding 2, please encourage him or her to practice adding 1 again.

■ Add the numbers below.

(1) $3 + 1 =$

(2) $5 + 1 =$

(3) $9 + 1 =$

(4) $10 + 1 =$

(5) $13 + 1 =$

(6) $4 + 2 =$

(7) $5 + 2 =$

(8) $8 + 2 =$

(9) $10 + 2 =$

(10) $14 + 2 =$

(11) $14 + 1 =$

(12) $19 + 1 =$

(13) $20 + 1 =$

(14) $23 + 1 =$

(15) $28 + 1 =$

(16) $15 + 2 =$

(17) $18 + 2 =$

(18) $20 + 2 =$

(19) $24 + 2 =$

(20) $28 + 2 =$

■ Add the numbers below.

(1) $6 + 1 =$

(2) $1 + 2 =$

(3) $3 + 1 =$

(4) $11 + 2 =$

(5) $7 + 1 =$

(6) $6 + 2 =$

(7) $15 + 1 =$

(8) $12 + 2 =$

(9) $12 + 1 =$

(10) $18 + 2 =$

(11) $16 + 1 =$

(12) $17 + 2 =$

(13) $24 + 1 =$

(14) $19 + 2 =$

(15) $21 + 1 =$

(16) $25 + 2 =$

(17) $25 + 1 =$

(18) $26 + 2 =$

(19) $29 + 1 =$

(20) $23 + 2 =$

Review
Adding 1 and 2

■ Add the numbers below.

(1) $9 + 1 =$

(2) $9 + 2 =$

(3) $10 + 2 =$

(4) $11 + 1 =$

(5) $14 + 1 =$

(6) $2 + 2 =$

(7) $8 + 1 =$

(8) $18 + 2 =$

(9) $24 + 2 =$

(10) $23 + 1 =$

(11) $4 + 1 =$

(12) $20 + 2 =$

(13) $27 + 1 =$

(14) $28 + 2 =$

(15) $13 + 2 =$

(16) $18 + 1 =$

(17) $20 + 1 =$

(18) $15 + 2 =$

(19) $26 + 1 =$

(20) $22 + 2 =$

■ Add the numbers below.

(1) $17 + 1 =$

(2) $21 + 2 =$

(3) $14 + 2 =$

(4) $10 + 1 =$

(5) $4 + 2 =$

(6) $28 + 1 =$

(7) $19 + 2 =$

(8) $1 + 1 =$

(9) $8 + 2 =$

(10) $22 + 1 =$

(11) $5 + 1 =$

(12) $13 + 1 =$

(13) $9 + 2 =$

(14) $3 + 2 =$

(15) $16 + 2 =$

(16) $2 + 1 =$

(17) $7 + 2 =$

(18) $19 + 1 =$

(19) $27 + 2 =$

(20) $29 + 1 =$

7

Adding 3
1+3 to 7+3

Name

Date

To parents

Starting with this page, your child will learn to add 3. If your child is having difficulty with adding 3, please encourage him or her to return to practice that includes adding 2 before proceeding.

■ Add the numbers below.

(1) $1 + 3 =$

(2) $2 + 3 =$

(3) $3 + 3 =$

(4) $4 + 3 =$

(5) $5 + 3 =$

(6) $6 + 3 =$

(7) $7 + 3 =$

(8) $1 + 3 =$

(9) $2 + 3 =$

(10) $4 + 3 =$

(11) $3 + 3 =$

(12) $5 + 3 =$

(13) $7 + 3 =$

(14) $6 + 3 =$

(15) $2 + 3 =$

(16) $3 + 3 =$

(17) $5 + 3 =$

(18) $4 + 3 =$

(19) $6 + 3 =$

(20) $7 + 3 =$

| 1 | 2 | 3 | 4 | 5 | 6 | 7 | 8 | 9 | 10 |

■ Add the numbers below.

(1) 4 + 3 =

(2) 6 + 3 =

(3) 7 + 3 =

(4) 2 + 3 =

(5) 5 + 3 =

(6) 3 + 3 =

(7) 1 + 3 =

(8) 4 + 3 =

(9) 7 + 3 =

(10) 3 + 3 =

(11) 5 + 3 =

(12) 6 + 3 =

(13) 1 + 3 =

(14) 2 + 3 =

(15) 4 + 3 =

(16) 6 + 3 =

(17) 1 + 3 =

(18) 7 + 3 =

(19) 3 + 3 =

(20) 5 + 3 =

| 1 | 2 | 3 | 4 | 5 | 6 | 7 | 8 | 9 | 10 |

8 Adding 3

8+3 to 17+3

Name

Date

■ Add the numbers below.

(1) $8 + 3 =$

(2) $9 + 3 =$

(3) $10 + 3 =$

(4) $11 + 3 =$

(5) $12 + 3 =$

(6) $13 + 3 =$

(7) $14 + 3 =$

(8) $15 + 3 =$

(9) $16 + 3 =$

(10) $17 + 3 =$

(11) $9 + 3 =$

(12) $10 + 3 =$

(13) $8 + 3 =$

(14) $14 + 3 =$

(15) $11 + 3 =$

(16) $12 + 3 =$

(17) $13 + 3 =$

(18) $17 + 3 =$

(19) $15 + 3 =$

(20) $16 + 3 =$

| 11 | 12 | 13 | 14 | 15 | 16 | 17 | 18 | 19 | 20 |

■ Add the numbers below.

(1) $15 + 3 =$

(2) $17 + 3 =$

(3) $9 + 3 =$

(4) $12 + 3 =$

(5) $8 + 3 =$

(6) $14 + 3 =$

(7) $11 + 3 =$

(8) $13 + 3 =$

(9) $16 + 3 =$

(10) $10 + 3 =$

(11) $9 + 3 =$

(12) $15 + 3 =$

(13) $17 + 3 =$

(14) $8 + 3 =$

(15) $11 + 3 =$

(16) $10 + 3 =$

(17) $13 + 3 =$

(18) $16 + 3 =$

(19) $14 + 3 =$

(20) $12 + 3 =$

11	12	13	14	15	16	17	18	19	20

Name
Date

■ Add the numbers below.

(1) $12 + 3 =$

(2) $15 + 3 =$

(3) $10 + 3 =$

(4) $16 + 3 =$

(5) $8 + 3 =$

(6) $13 + 3 =$

(7) $11 + 3 =$

(8) $17 + 3 =$

(9) $14 + 3 =$

(10) $9 + 3 =$

(11) $12 + 3 =$

(12) $8 + 3 =$

(13) $14 + 3 =$

(14) $17 + 3 =$

(15) $11 + 3 =$

(16) $15 + 3 =$

(17) $9 + 3 =$

(18) $16 + 3 =$

(19) $13 + 3 =$

(20) $10 + 3 =$

11 12 13 14 15 16 17 18 19 20

1+3 to 17+3

■ Add the numbers below.

(1) $6 + 3 =$

(2) $14 + 3 =$

(3) $17 + 3 =$

(4) $9 + 3 =$

(5) $1 + 3 =$

(6) $11 + 3 =$

(7) $13 + 3 =$

(8) $2 + 3 =$

(9) $7 + 3 =$

(10) $17 + 3 =$

(11) $8 + 3 =$

(12) $3 + 3 =$

(13) $15 + 3 =$

(14) $5 + 3 =$

(15) $10 + 3 =$

(16) $1 + 3 =$

(17) $16 + 3 =$

(18) $4 + 3 =$

(19) $12 + 3 =$

(20) $2 + 3 =$

| 1 | 2 | 3 | 4 | 5 | 6 | 7 | 8 | 9 | 10 | 11 | 12 | 13 | 14 | 15 | 16 | 17 | 18 | 19 | 20 |

10 Adding 4
1+4 to 6+4

Name

Date

To parents
Starting with this page, your child will learn to add 4. If your child is having difficulty with adding 4, please encourage him or her to return to practice that includes adding 3 before proceeding.

■ Add the numbers below.

(1) $1 + 4 =$

(2) $2 + 4 =$

(3) $3 + 4 =$

(4) $4 + 4 =$

(5) $5 + 4 =$

(6) $6 + 4 =$

(7) $1 + 4 =$

(8) $2 + 4 =$

(9) $4 + 4 =$

(10) $3 + 4 =$

(11) $5 + 4 =$

(12) $6 + 4 =$

(13) $1 + 4 =$

(14) $3 + 4 =$

(15) $2 + 4 =$

(16) $6 + 4 =$

(17) $4 + 4 =$

(18) $5 + 4 =$

(19) $3 + 4 =$

(20) $6 + 4 =$

1 2 3 4 5 6 7 8 9 10

■ Add the numbers below.

(1) $1 + 4 =$

(2) $6 + 4 =$

(3) $3 + 4 =$

(4) $2 + 4 =$

(5) $5 + 4 =$

(6) $4 + 4 =$

(7) $1 + 4 =$

(8) $2 + 4 =$

(9) $5 + 4 =$

(10) $6 + 4 =$

(11) $4 + 4 =$

(12) $3 + 4 =$

(13) $2 + 4 =$

(14) $4 + 4 =$

(15) $6 + 4 =$

(16) $5 + 4 =$

(17) $1 + 4 =$

(18) $3 + 4 =$

(19) $5 + 4 =$

(20) $4 + 4 =$

| 1 | 2 | 3 | 4 | 5 | 6 | 7 | 8 | 9 | 10 |

Adding 4
7+4 to 16+4

Name

Date

■ Add the numbers below.

(1)　　7 + 4 =

(2)　　8 + 4 =

(3)　　9 + 4 =

(4)　10 + 4 =

(5)　11 + 4 =

(6)　12 + 4 =

(7)　13 + 4 =

(8)　14 + 4 =

(9)　15 + 4 =

(10)　16 + 4 =

(11)　　9 + 4 =

(12)　　7 + 4 =

(13)　　8 + 4 =

(14)　11 + 4 =

(15)　10 + 4 =

(16)　12 + 4 =

(17)　14 + 4 =

(18)　15 + 4 =

(19)　13 + 4 =

(20)　16 + 4 =

11 12 13 14 15 16 17 18 19 20

■ Add the numbers below.

(1) $11 + 4 =$

(2) $15 + 4 =$

(3) $16 + 4 =$

(4) $7 + 4 =$

(5) $10 + 4 =$

(6) $8 + 4 =$

(7) $9 + 4 =$

(8) $12 + 4 =$

(9) $14 + 4 =$

(10) $13 + 4 =$

(11) $12 + 4 =$

(12) $9 + 4 =$

(13) $8 + 4 =$

(14) $11 + 4 =$

(15) $16 + 4 =$

(16) $10 + 4 =$

(17) $15 + 4 =$

(18) $13 + 4 =$

(19) $7 + 4 =$

(20) $14 + 4 =$

| 11 | 12 | 13 | 14 | 15 | 16 | 17 | 18 | 19 | 20 |

Name
Date

■ Add the numbers below.

(1) $10 + 4 =$

(2) $8 + 4 =$

(3) $12 + 4 =$

(4) $16 + 4 =$

(5) $9 + 4 =$

(6) $14 + 4 =$

(7) $7 + 4 =$

(8) $15 + 4 =$

(9) $11 + 4 =$

(10) $13 + 4 =$

(11) $16 + 4 =$

(12) $7 + 4 =$

(13) $15 + 4 =$

(14) $11 + 4 =$

(15) $9 + 4 =$

(16) $12 + 4 =$

(17) $13 + 4 =$

(18) $10 + 4 =$

(19) $14 + 4 =$

(20) $8 + 4 =$

| 11 | 12 | 13 | 14 | 15 | 16 | 17 | 18 | 19 | 20 |

1+4 to 16+4

■ Add the numbers below.

(1) $5 + 4 =$

(2) $11 + 4 =$

(3) $7 + 4 =$

(4) $14 + 4 =$

(5) $8 + 4 =$

(6) $1 + 4 =$

(7) $16 + 4 =$

(8) $3 + 4 =$

(9) $9 + 4 =$

(10) $15 + 4 =$

(11) $8 + 4 =$

(12) $10 + 4 =$

(13) $13 + 4 =$

(14) $4 + 4 =$

(15) $6 + 4 =$

(16) $7 + 4 =$

(17) $2 + 4 =$

(18) $9 + 4 =$

(19) $12 + 4 =$

(20) $16 + 4 =$

| 1 | 2 | 3 | 4 | 5 | 6 | 7 | 8 | 9 | 10 | 11 | 12 | 13 | 14 | 15 | 16 | 17 | 18 | 19 | 20 |

13 Review
Adding 3 and 4

Name

Date

To parents
Starting with this page, your child will review addition that includes the numbers 3 and 4. If he or she is having difficulty solving problems that include adding 3, please encourage him or her to practice adding 2 again. Likewise, if he or she is having difficulty with adding 4, please encourage him or her to practice adding 3 again.

■ Add the numbers below.

(1) $2 + 3 =$

(2) $3 + 3 =$

(3) $1 + 3 =$

(4) $4 + 3 =$

(5) $2 + 4 =$

(6) $1 + 4 =$

(7) $3 + 4 =$

(8) $5 + 3 =$

(9) $6 + 3 =$

(10) $7 + 3 =$

(11) $5 + 4 =$

(12) $4 + 4 =$

(13) $6 + 4 =$

(14) $6 + 3 =$

(15) $5 + 3 =$

(16) $7 + 3 =$

(17) $2 + 4 =$

(18) $1 + 4 =$

(19) $5 + 4 =$

(20) $6 + 4 =$

■ Add the numbers below.

(1) $8 + 3 =$

(2) $7 + 4 =$

(3) $9 + 3 =$

(4) $8 + 4 =$

(5) $10 + 3 =$

(6) $9 + 4 =$

(7) $11 + 3 =$

(8) $10 + 4 =$

(9) $12 + 3 =$

(10) $11 + 4 =$

(11) $13 + 3 =$

(12) $12 + 4 =$

(13) $14 + 3 =$

(14) $13 + 4 =$

(15) $15 + 3 =$

(16) $14 + 4 =$

(17) $16 + 3 =$

(18) $15 + 4 =$

(19) $17 + 3 =$

(20) $16 + 4 =$

14 Review
Adding 3 and 4

■ Add the numbers below.

(1) $8 + 3 =$

(2) $10 + 3 =$

(3) $10 + 4 =$

(4) $13 + 4 =$

(5) $1 + 4 =$

(6) $1 + 3 =$

(7) $7 + 4 =$

(8) $9 + 3 =$

(9) $16 + 3 =$

(10) $12 + 4 =$

(11) $4 + 4 =$

(12) $5 + 3 =$

(13) $14 + 3 =$

(14) $17 + 3 =$

(15) $11 + 4 =$

(16) $14 + 4 =$

(17) $15 + 3 =$

(18) $15 + 4 =$

(19) $6 + 3 =$

(20) $16 + 4 =$

■ Add the numbers below.

(1)   3 + 3 =

(2)   3 + 4 =

(3)   11 + 4 =

(4)   12 + 3 =

(5)   4 + 3 =

(6)   10 + 4 =

(7)   13 + 3 =

(8)   12 + 4 =

(9)   2 + 4 =

(10)   2 + 3 =

(11)   17 + 3 =

(12)   8 + 4 =

(13)   7 + 3 =

(14)   13 + 4 =

(15)   14 + 4 =

(16)   8 + 3 =

(17)   9 + 3 =

(18)   9 + 4 =

(19)   11 + 3 =

(20)   15 + 4 =

Review
Adding 1 to 4

Name

Date

To parents
Starting with this page, your child will review addition that includes numbers up to 4. If he or she is having difficulty, please encourage him or her to return to the previous stages.

■ Add the numbers below.

(1) $2 + 1 =$

(2) $2 + 2 =$

(3) $1 + 3 =$

(4) $1 + 4 =$

(5) $7 + 1 =$

(6) $3 + 2 =$

(7) $2 + 3 =$

(8) $4 + 4 =$

(9) $14 + 1 =$

(10) $4 + 2 =$

(11) $8 + 3 =$

(12) $7 + 4 =$

(13) $22 + 1 =$

(14) $5 + 2 =$

(15) $12 + 3 =$

(16) $10 + 4 =$

(17) $26 + 1 =$

(18) $6 + 2 =$

(19) $16 + 3 =$

(20) $12 + 4 =$

■ Add the numbers below.

(1) $5 + 1 =$

(2) $3 + 2 =$

(3) $3 + 3 =$

(4) $2 + 4 =$

(5) $7 + 2 =$

(6) $6 + 1 =$

(7) $5 + 4 =$

(8) $6 + 3 =$

(9) $9 + 3 =$

(10) $13 + 1 =$

(11) $13 + 2 =$

(12) $8 + 4 =$

(13) $13 + 4 =$

(14) $22 + 2 =$

(15) $20 + 1 =$

(16) $13 + 3 =$

(17) $27 + 2 =$

(18) $15 + 4 =$

(19) $28 + 1 =$

(20) $14 + 3 =$

16 Review
Adding 1 to 4

Name	
Date	

■ Add the numbers below.

(1) $2 + 2 =$

(2) $9 + 3 =$

(3) $9 + 4 =$

(4) $3 + 1 =$

(5) $3 + 4 =$

(6) $12 + 2 =$

(7) $8 + 3 =$

(8) $21 + 1 =$

(9) $7 + 4 =$

(10) $6 + 2 =$

(11) $7 + 3 =$

(12) $24 + 1 =$

(13) $10 + 3 =$

(14) $8 + 1 =$

(15) $14 + 4 =$

(16) $25 + 2 =$

(17) $15 + 1 =$

(18) $15 + 3 =$

(19) $19 + 2 =$

(20) $16 + 4 =$

■ Add the numbers below.

(1) $12 + 1 =$

(2) $16 + 4 =$

(3) $11 + 3 =$

(4) $11 + 2 =$

(5) $6 + 4 =$

(6) $18 + 1 =$

(7) $23 + 2 =$

(8) $4 + 3 =$

(9) $10 + 4 =$

(10) $4 + 1 =$

(11) $5 + 2 =$

(12) $17 + 3 =$

(13) $17 + 1 =$

(14) $28 + 2 =$

(15) $12 + 4 =$

(16) $25 + 1 =$

(17) $5 + 3 =$

(18) $9 + 4 =$

(19) $17 + 2 =$

(20) $7 + 3 =$

Adding 5

17 1+5 to 5+5

Name

Date

To parents
Starting with this page, your child will learn to add 5. If he or she is having difficulty with adding 5, please encourage him or her to return to practice that includes adding 4 before proceeding.

■ Add the numbers below.

(1) $1 + 5 =$

(2) $2 + 5 =$

(3) $3 + 5 =$

(4) $4 + 5 =$

(5) $5 + 5 =$

(6) $2 + 5 =$

(7) $3 + 5 =$

(8) $1 + 5 =$

(9) $4 + 5 =$

(10) $5 + 5 =$

(11) $3 + 5 =$

(12) $2 + 5 =$

(13) $1 + 5 =$

(14) $5 + 5 =$

(15) $4 + 5 =$

(16) $1 + 5 =$

(17) $4 + 5 =$

(18) $2 + 5 =$

(19) $5 + 5 =$

(20) $3 + 5 =$

| 1 | 2 | 3 | 4 | 5 | 6 | 7 | 8 | 9 | 10 |

6+5 to 10+5

■ Add the numbers below.

(1)　　6 + 5 =　　　　　　(11)　　7 + 5 =

(2)　　7 + 5 =　　　　　　(12)　　6 + 5 =

(3)　　8 + 5 =　　　　　　(13)　　9 + 5 =

(4)　　9 + 5 =　　　　　　(14)　　8 + 5 =

(5)　10 + 5 =　　　　　　(15)　10 + 5 =

(6)　　6 + 5 =　　　　　　(16)　　8 + 5 =

(7)　　8 + 5 =　　　　　　(17)　　7 + 5 =

(8)　　7 + 5 =　　　　　　(18)　　6 + 5 =

(9)　　9 + 5 =　　　　　　(19)　10 + 5 =

(10)　10 + 5 =　　　　　　(20)　　9 + 5 =

| 11 | 12 | 13 | 14 | 15 |

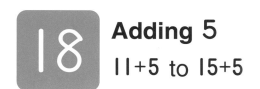

Adding 5

11+5 to 15+5

■ Add the numbers below.

(1) 11 + 5 =

(2) 12 + 5 =

(3) 13 + 5 =

(4) 14 + 5 =

(5) 15 + 5 =

(6) 12 + 5 =

(7) 11 + 5 =

(8) 13 + 5 =

(9) 14 + 5 =

(10) 15 + 5 =

(11) 12 + 5 =

(12) 11 + 5 =

(13) 13 + 5 =

(14) 15 + 5 =

(15) 14 + 5 =

(16) 13 + 5 =

(17) 11 + 5 =

(18) 12 + 5 =

(19) 15 + 5 =

(20) 14 + 5 =

11	12	13	14	15	16	17	18	19	20

1+5 to 15+5

■ Add the numbers below.

(1) $2 + 5 =$

(2) $1 + 5 =$

(3) $5 + 5 =$

(4) $4 + 5 =$

(5) $6 + 5 =$

(6) $3 + 5 =$

(7) $7 + 5 =$

(8) $9 + 5 =$

(9) $10 + 5 =$

(10) $8 + 5 =$

(11) $11 + 5 =$

(12) $14 + 5 =$

(13) $15 + 5 =$

(14) $12 + 5 =$

(15) $13 + 5 =$

(16) $1 + 5 =$

(17) $5 + 5 =$

(18) $11 + 5 =$

(19) $10 + 5 =$

(20) $13 + 5 =$

| 1 | 2 | 3 | 4 | 5 | 6 | 7 | 8 | 9 | 10 | 11 | 12 | 13 | 14 | 15 | 16 | 17 | 18 | 19 | 20 |

19 Adding 5
1+5 to 15+5

Name

Date

■ Add the numbers below.

(1) $3 + 5 =$

(2) $6 + 5 =$

(3) $12 + 5 =$

(4) $1 + 5 =$

(5) $8 + 5 =$

(6) $2 + 5 =$

(7) $10 + 5 =$

(8) $4 + 5 =$

(9) $11 + 5 =$

(10) $5 + 5 =$

(11) $14 + 5 =$

(12) $7 + 5 =$

(13) $13 + 5 =$

(14) $9 + 5 =$

(15) $15 + 5 =$

(16) $2 + 5 =$

(17) $6 + 5 =$

(18) $14 + 5 =$

(19) $3 + 5 =$

(20) $8 + 5 =$

| 1 | 2 | 3 | 4 | 5 | 6 | 7 | 8 | 9 | 10 | 11 | 12 | 13 | 14 | 15 | 16 | 17 | 18 | 19 | 20 |

■ Add the numbers below.

(1)　　7 + 5 =

(2)　12 + 5 =

(3)　14 + 5 =

(4)　　6 + 5 =

(5)　　9 + 5 =

(6)　　3 + 5 =

(7)　15 + 5 =

(8)　　4 + 5 =

(9)　10 + 5 =

(10)　　1 + 5 =

(11)　　8 + 5 =

(12)　　5 + 5 =

(13)　11 + 5 =

(14)　13 + 5 =

(15)　　2 + 5 =

(16)　15 + 5 =

(17)　　7 + 5 =

(18)　　9 + 5 =

(19)　　4 + 5 =

(20)　12 + 5 =

| 1 | 2 | 3 | 4 | 5 | 6 | 7 | 8 | 9 | 10 | 11 | 12 | 13 | 14 | 15 | 16 | 17 | 18 | 19 | 20 |

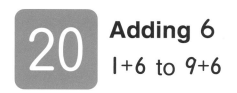

Adding 6

1+6 to 9+6

Name

Date

To parents
Starting with this page, your child will learn to add 6. If he or she is having difficulty with adding 6, please encourage him or her to return to practice that includes adding 5 before proceeding.

■ Add the numbers below.

(1) 1 + 6 =

(2) 2 + 6 =

(3) 3 + 6 =

(4) 4 + 6 =

(5) 5 + 6 =

(6) 6 + 6 =

(7) 7 + 6 =

(8) 8 + 6 =

(9) 9 + 6 =

(10) 2 + 6 =

(11) 3 + 6 =

(12) 4 + 6 =

(13) 1 + 6 =

(14) 6 + 6 =

(15) 7 + 6 =

(16) 5 + 6 =

(17) 9 + 6 =

(18) 8 + 6 =

(19) 3 + 6 =

(20) 4 + 6 =

| 1 | 2 | 3 | 4 | 5 | 6 | 7 | 8 | 9 | 10 | 11 | 12 | 13 | 14 | 15 |

5+6 to 14+6

■ Add the numbers below.

(1)　　5 + 6 =

(2)　　6 + 6 =

(3)　　7 + 6 =

(4)　　8 + 6 =

(5)　　9 + 6 =

(6)　10 + 6 =

(7)　11 + 6 =

(8)　12 + 6 =

(9)　13 + 6 =

(10)　14 + 6 =

(11)　11 + 6 =

(12)　10 + 6 =

(13)　13 + 6 =

(14)　12 + 6 =

(15)　14 + 6 =

(16)　10 + 6 =

(17)　13 + 6 =

(18)　11 + 6 =

(19)　14 + 6 =

(20)　12 + 6 =

| 11 | 12 | 13 | 14 | 15 | 16 | 17 | 18 | 19 | 20 |

21 Adding 6

1+6 to 14+6

Name

Date

■ Add the numbers below.

(1) $3 + 6 =$

(2) $2 + 6 =$

(3) $1 + 6 =$

(4) $4 + 6 =$

(5) $6 + 6 =$

(6) $5 + 6 =$

(7) $8 + 6 =$

(8) $7 + 6 =$

(9) $9 + 6 =$

(10) $11 + 6 =$

(11) $10 + 6 =$

(12) $13 + 6 =$

(13) $12 + 6 =$

(14) $14 + 6 =$

(15) $1 + 6 =$

(16) $4 + 6 =$

(17) $2 + 6 =$

(18) $3 + 6 =$

(19) $6 + 6 =$

(20) $5 + 6 =$

| 1 | 2 | 3 | 4 | 5 | 6 | 7 | 8 | 9 | 10 | 11 | 12 | 13 | 14 | 15 | 16 | 17 | 18 | 19 | 20 |

■ Add the numbers below.

(1)   7 + 6 =

(2)   9 + 6 =

(3)   6 + 6 =

(4)   3 + 6 =

(5)   8 + 6 =

(6)   11 + 6 =

(7)   1 + 6 =

(8)   2 + 6 =

(9)   5 + 6 =

(10)   14 + 6 =

(11)   12 + 6 =

(12)   13 + 6 =

(13)   4 + 6 =

(14)   10 + 6 =

(15)   7 + 6 =

(16)   12 + 6 =

(17)   9 + 6 =

(18)   10 + 6 =

(19)   11 + 6 =

(20)   8 + 6 =

| 1 | 2 | 3 | 4 | 5 | 6 | 7 | 8 | 9 | 10 | 11 | 12 | 13 | 14 | 15 | 16 | 17 | 18 | 19 | 20 |

Name

Date

■ Add the numbers below.

(1)   5 + 6 =

(2)   9 + 6 =

(3)   13 + 6 =

(4)   2 + 6 =

(5)   8 + 6 =

(6)   14 + 6 =

(7)   6 + 6 =

(8)   12 + 6 =

(9)   3 + 6 =

(10)   11 + 6 =

(11)   7 + 6 =

(12)   10 + 6 =

(13)   1 + 6 =

(14)   4 + 6 =

(15)   14 + 6 =

(16)   5 + 6 =

(17)   13 + 6 =

(18)   4 + 6 =

(19)   10 + 6 =

(20)   6 + 6 =

| 1 | 2 | 3 | 4 | 5 | 6 | 7 | 8 | 9 | 10 | 11 | 12 | 13 | 14 | 15 | 16 | 17 | 18 | 19 | 20 |

■ Add the numbers below.

(1) $9 + 6 =$

(2) $13 + 6 =$

(3) $7 + 6 =$

(4) $11 + 6 =$

(5) $14 + 6 =$

(6) $5 + 6 =$

(7) $3 + 6 =$

(8) $8 + 6 =$

(9) $6 + 6 =$

(10) $2 + 6 =$

(11) $12 + 6 =$

(12) $4 + 6 =$

(13) $10 + 6 =$

(14) $1 + 6 =$

(15) $7 + 6 =$

(16) $2 + 6 =$

(17) $14 + 6 =$

(18) $8 + 6 =$

(19) $1 + 6 =$

(20) $9 + 6 =$

| 1 | 2 | 3 | 4 | 5 | 6 | 7 | 8 | 9 | 10 | 11 | 12 | 13 | 14 | 15 | 16 | 17 | 18 | 19 | 20 |

23 Review
Adding 5 and 6

Name

Date

To parents
Starting with this page, your child will review addition that includes the numbers 5 and 6. If he or she is having difficulty solving problems that include adding 5, please encourage him or her to practice adding 4 again. Likewise, if he or she is having difficulty with adding 6, please encourage him or her to practice adding 5 again.

■ Add the numbers below.

(1) $1 + 5 =$

(2) $3 + 5 =$

(3) $4 + 5 =$

(4) $5 + 5 =$

(5) $6 + 5 =$

(6) $1 + 6 =$

(7) $2 + 6 =$

(8) $3 + 6 =$

(9) $4 + 6 =$

(10) $6 + 6 =$

(11) $7 + 5 =$

(12) $11 + 5 =$

(13) $10 + 5 =$

(14) $12 + 5 =$

(15) $15 + 5 =$

(16) $7 + 6 =$

(17) $9 + 6 =$

(18) $10 + 6 =$

(19) $12 + 6 =$

(20) $13 + 6 =$

■ Add the numbers below.

(1) 2 + 5 =

(2) 3 + 6 =

(3) 3 + 5 =

(4) 5 + 6 =

(5) 7 + 5 =

(6) 6 + 6 =

(7) 8 + 5 =

(8) 8 + 6 =

(9) 9 + 5 =

(10) 7 + 6 =

(11) 15 + 5 =

(12) 9 + 6 =

(13) 11 + 5 =

(14) 11 + 6 =

(15) 12 + 5 =

(16) 12 + 6 =

(17) 14 + 5 =

(18) 13 + 6 =

(19) 13 + 5 =

(20) 14 + 6 =

24 Review
Adding 5 and 6

Name

Date

■ Add the numbers below.

(1) $1 + 5 =$

(2) $4 + 6 =$

(3) $1 + 6 =$

(4) $5 + 6 =$

(5) $2 + 5 =$

(6) $5 + 5 =$

(7) $8 + 5 =$

(8) $4 + 5 =$

(9) $8 + 6 =$

(10) $6 + 5 =$

(11) $3 + 6 =$

(12) $7 + 6 =$

(13) $10 + 5 =$

(14) $10 + 6 =$

(15) $12 + 6 =$

(16) $9 + 5 =$

(17) $14 + 5 =$

(18) $14 + 6 =$

(19) $11 + 6 =$

(20) $13 + 5 =$

■ Add the numbers below.

(1) $7 + 5 =$

(2) $6 + 6 =$

(3) $2 + 6 =$

(4) $2 + 5 =$

(5) $5 + 6 =$

(6) $11 + 6 =$

(7) $3 + 5 =$

(8) $1 + 6 =$

(9) $9 + 6 =$

(10) $11 + 5 =$

(11) $1 + 5 =$

(12) $15 + 5 =$

(13) $4 + 6 =$

(14) $8 + 6 =$

(15) $4 + 5 =$

(16) $14 + 6 =$

(17) $13 + 6 =$

(18) $14 + 5 =$

(19) $9 + 5 =$

(20) $13 + 5 =$

Adding 7

1+7 to 8+7

Name

Date

To parents
Starting with this page, your child will learn to add 7. If he or she is having difficulty with adding 7, please encourage him or her to return to practice that includes adding 6 before proceeding.

■ Add the numbers below.

(1) $1 + 7 =$

(2) $2 + 7 =$

(3) $3 + 7 =$

(4) $4 + 7 =$

(5) $5 + 7 =$

(6) $6 + 7 =$

(7) $7 + 7 =$

(8) $8 + 7 =$

(9) $1 + 7 =$

(10) $2 + 7 =$

(11) $5 + 7 =$

(12) $3 + 7 =$

(13) $4 + 7 =$

(14) $6 + 7 =$

(15) $8 + 7 =$

(16) $7 + 7 =$

(17) $2 + 7 =$

(18) $3 + 7 =$

(19) $1 + 7 =$

(20) $4 + 7 =$

| 1 | 2 | 3 | 4 | 5 | 6 | 7 | 8 | 9 | 10 | 11 | 12 | 13 | 14 | 15 |

4+7 to 13+7

■ Add the numbers below.

(1) $4 + 7 =$

(2) $5 + 7 =$

(3) $6 + 7 =$

(4) $7 + 7 =$

(5) $8 + 7 =$

(6) $9 + 7 =$

(7) $10 + 7 =$

(8) $11 + 7 =$

(9) $12 + 7 =$

(10) $13 + 7 =$

(11) $9 + 7 =$

(12) $11 + 7 =$

(13) $10 + 7 =$

(14) $12 + 7 =$

(15) $13 + 7 =$

(16) $10 + 7 =$

(17) $11 + 7 =$

(18) $9 + 7 =$

(19) $13 + 7 =$

(20) $12 + 7 =$

11 12 13 14 15 16 17 18 19 20

Name
Date

■ Add the numbers below.

(1) $1 + 7 =$

(2) $2 + 7 =$

(3) $3 + 7 =$

(4) $4 + 7 =$

(5) $5 + 7 =$

(6) $6 + 7 =$

(7) $7 + 7 =$

(8) $8 + 7 =$

(9) $9 + 7 =$

(10) $10 + 7 =$

(11) $11 + 7 =$

(12) $12 + 7 =$

(13) $13 + 7 =$

(14) $1 + 7 =$

(15) $3 + 7 =$

(16) $2 + 7 =$

(17) $5 + 7 =$

(18) $4 + 7 =$

(19) $6 + 7 =$

(20) $7 + 7 =$

| 1 | 2 | 3 | 4 | 5 | 6 | 7 | 8 | 9 | 10 | 11 | 12 | 13 | 14 | 15 | 16 | 17 | 18 | 19 | 20 |

Add the numbers below.

(1) $1 + 7 =$

(2) $3 + 7 =$

(3) $2 + 7 =$

(4) $5 + 7 =$

(5) $4 + 7 =$

(6) $6 + 7 =$

(7) $8 + 7 =$

(8) $7 + 7 =$

(9) $10 + 7 =$

(10) $9 + 7 =$

(11) $11 + 7 =$

(12) $13 + 7 =$

(13) $12 + 7 =$

(14) $7 + 7 =$

(15) $9 + 7 =$

(16) $8 + 7 =$

(17) $11 + 7 =$

(18) $10 + 7 =$

(19) $12 + 7 =$

(20) $13 + 7 =$

| 1 | 2 | 3 | 4 | 5 | 6 | 7 | 8 | 9 | 10 | 11 | 12 | 13 | 14 | 15 | 16 | 17 | 18 | 19 | 20 |

27 **Adding 7**
1+7 to 13+7

Name

Date

■ Add the numbers below.

(1) $3 + 7 =$

(2) $11 + 7 =$

(3) $6 + 7 =$

(4) $1 + 7 =$

(5) $12 + 7 =$

(6) $5 + 7 =$

(7) $10 + 7 =$

(8) $2 + 7 =$

(9) $7 + 7 =$

(10) $13 + 7 =$

(11) $4 + 7 =$

(12) $8 + 7 =$

(13) $9 + 7 =$

(14) $3 + 7 =$

(15) $12 + 7 =$

(16) $6 + 7 =$

(17) $5 + 7 =$

(18) $11 + 7 =$

(19) $7 + 7 =$

(20) $10 + 7 =$

| 1 | 2 | 3 | 4 | 5 | 6 | 7 | 8 | 9 | 10 | 11 | 12 | 13 | 14 | 15 | 16 | 17 | 18 | 19 | 20 |

■ Add the numbers below.

(1) $6 + 7 =$

(2) $12 + 7 =$

(3) $2 + 7 =$

(4) $8 + 7 =$

(5) $4 + 7 =$

(6) $13 + 7 =$

(7) $7 + 7 =$

(8) $9 + 7 =$

(9) $1 + 7 =$

(10) $5 + 7 =$

(11) $11 + 7 =$

(12) $3 + 7 =$

(13) $10 + 7 =$

(14) $2 + 7 =$

(15) $9 + 7 =$

(16) $4 + 7 =$

(17) $13 + 7 =$

(18) $6 + 7 =$

(19) $8 + 7 =$

(20) $1 + 7 =$

| 1 | 2 | 3 | 4 | 5 | 6 | 7 | 8 | 9 | 10 | 11 | 12 | 13 | 14 | 15 | 16 | 17 | 18 | 19 | 20 |

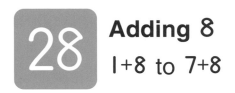

Adding 8

1+8 to 7+8

Name

Date

To parents
Starting with this page, your child will learn to add 8. If he or she is having difficulty with adding 8, please encourage him or her to return to practice that includes adding 7 before proceeding.

■ Add the numbers below.

(1) $1 + 8 =$

(2) $2 + 8 =$

(3) $3 + 8 =$

(4) $4 + 8 =$

(5) $5 + 8 =$

(6) $6 + 8 =$

(7) $7 + 8 =$

(8) $1 + 8 =$

(9) $3 + 8 =$

(10) $2 + 8 =$

(11) $4 + 8 =$

(12) $5 + 8 =$

(13) $7 + 8 =$

(14) $6 + 8 =$

(15) $2 + 8 =$

(16) $1 + 8 =$

(17) $3 + 8 =$

(18) $5 + 8 =$

(19) $4 + 8 =$

(20) $6 + 8 =$

| 1 | 2 | 3 | 4 | 5 | 6 | 7 | 8 | 9 | 10 | 11 | 12 | 13 | 14 | 15 |

3+8 to 12+8

■ Add the numbers below.

(1) $3 + 8 =$

(2) $4 + 8 =$

(3) $5 + 8 =$

(4) $6 + 8 =$

(5) $7 + 8 =$

(6) $8 + 8 =$

(7) $9 + 8 =$

(8) $10 + 8 =$

(9) $11 + 8 =$

(10) $12 + 8 =$

(11) $8 + 8 =$

(12) $9 + 8 =$

(13) $11 + 8 =$

(14) $10 + 8 =$

(15) $12 + 8 =$

(16) $9 + 8 =$

(17) $8 + 8 =$

(18) $10 + 8 =$

(19) $12 + 8 =$

(20) $11 + 8 =$

| 11 | 12 | 13 | 14 | 15 | 16 | 17 | 18 | 19 | 20 |

Name	
Date	

■ Add the numbers below.

(1) 1 + 8 =

(2) 2 + 8 =

(3) 3 + 8 =

(4) 4 + 8 =

(5) 5 + 8 =

(6) 6 + 8 =

(7) 7 + 8 =

(8) 8 + 8 =

(9) 9 + 8 =

(10) 10 + 8 =

(11) 11 + 8 =

(12) 12 + 8 =

(13) 1 + 8 =

(14) 2 + 8 =

(15) 7 + 8 =

(16) 8 + 8 =

(17) 10 + 8 =

(18) 9 + 8 =

(19) 11 + 8 =

(20) 12 + 8 =

| 1 | 2 | 3 | 4 | 5 | 6 | 7 | 8 | 9 | 10 | 11 | 12 | 13 | 14 | 15 | 16 | 17 | 18 | 19 | 20 |

■ Add the numbers below.

(1) $1 + 8 =$

(2) $2 + 8 =$

(3) $4 + 8 =$

(4) $3 + 8 =$

(5) $5 + 8 =$

(6) $7 + 8 =$

(7) $6 + 8 =$

(8) $8 + 8 =$

(9) $10 + 8 =$

(10) $9 + 8 =$

(11) $11 + 8 =$

(12) $12 + 8 =$

(13) $3 + 8 =$

(14) $2 + 8 =$

(15) $4 + 8 =$

(16) $5 + 8 =$

(17) $7 + 8 =$

(18) $6 + 8 =$

(19) $8 + 8 =$

(20) $9 + 8 =$

| 1 | 2 | 3 | 4 | 5 | 6 | 7 | 8 | 9 | 10 | 11 | 12 | 13 | 14 | 15 | 16 | 17 | 18 | 19 | 20 |

Adding 8

1+8 to 12+8

■ Add the numbers below.

(1) 5 + 8 =

(2) 6 + 8 =

(3) 11 + 8 =

(4) 1 + 8 =

(5) 2 + 8 =

(6) 7 + 8 =

(7) 9 + 8 =

(8) 3 + 8 =

(9) 10 + 8 =

(10) 4 + 8 =

(11) 12 + 8 =

(12) 8 + 8 =

(13) 1 + 8 =

(14) 6 + 8 =

(15) 12 + 8 =

(16) 3 + 8 =

(17) 11 + 8 =

(18) 8 + 8 =

(19) 10 + 8 =

(20) 4 + 8 =

| 1 | 2 | 3 | 4 | 5 | 6 | 7 | 8 | 9 | 10 | 11 | 12 | 13 | 14 | 15 | 16 | 17 | 18 | 19 | 20 |

■ Add the numbers below.

(1) $1 + 8 =$

(2) $8 + 8 =$

(3) $2 + 8 =$

(4) $12 + 8 =$

(5) $3 + 8 =$

(6) $7 + 8 =$

(7) $4 + 8 =$

(8) $10 + 8 =$

(9) $5 + 8 =$

(10) $6 + 8 =$

(11) $11 + 8 =$

(12) $9 + 8 =$

(13) $5 + 8 =$

(14) $12 + 8 =$

(15) $9 + 8 =$

(16) $2 + 8 =$

(17) $11 + 8 =$

(18) $10 + 8 =$

(19) $7 + 8 =$

(20) $1 + 8 =$

| 1 | 2 | 3 | 4 | 5 | 6 | 7 | 8 | 9 | 10 | 11 | 12 | 13 | 14 | 15 | 16 | 17 | 18 | 19 | 20 |

1+8 to 12+8

Adding 9

1+9 to 6+9

Name

Date

To parents
Starting with this page, your child will learn to add 9. If he or she is having difficulty with adding 9, please encourage him or her to return to practice that includes adding 8 before proceeding.

■ Add the numbers below.

(1) $1 + 9 =$

(2) $2 + 9 =$

(3) $3 + 9 =$

(4) $4 + 9 =$

(5) $5 + 9 =$

(6) $6 + 9 =$

(7) $1 + 9 =$

(8) $2 + 9 =$

(9) $4 + 9 =$

(10) $3 + 9 =$

(11) $5 + 9 =$

(12) $6 + 9 =$

(13) $2 + 9 =$

(14) $4 + 9 =$

(15) $1 + 9 =$

(16) $3 + 9 =$

(17) $5 + 9 =$

(18) $6 + 9 =$

(19) $1 + 9 =$

(20) $4 + 9 =$

| 1 | 2 | 3 | 4 | 5 | 6 | 7 | 8 | 9 | 10 | 11 | 12 | 13 | 14 | 15 |

2+9 to 11+9

■ Add the numbers below.

(1) $2 + 9 =$

(2) $3 + 9 =$

(3) $4 + 9 =$

(4) $5 + 9 =$

(5) $6 + 9 =$

(6) $7 + 9 =$

(7) $8 + 9 =$

(8) $9 + 9 =$

(9) $10 + 9 =$

(10) $11 + 9 =$

(11) $7 + 9 =$

(12) $8 + 9 =$

(13) $9 + 9 =$

(14) $11 + 9 =$

(15) $10 + 9 =$

(16) $8 + 9 =$

(17) $7 + 9 =$

(18) $9 + 9 =$

(19) $10 + 9 =$

(20) $11 + 9 =$

| 11 | 12 | 13 | 14 | 15 | 16 | 17 | 18 | 19 | 20 |

Name	
Date	

■ Add the numbers below.

(1) $1 + 9 =$

(2) $2 + 9 =$

(3) $3 + 9 =$

(4) $4 + 9 =$

(5) $5 + 9 =$

(6) $6 + 9 =$

(7) $7 + 9 =$

(8) $8 + 9 =$

(9) $9 + 9 =$

(10) $10 + 9 =$

(11) $11 + 9 =$

(12) $1 + 9 =$

(13) $3 + 9 =$

(14) $2 + 9 =$

(15) $5 + 9 =$

(16) $7 + 9 =$

(17) $9 + 9 =$

(18) $8 + 9 =$

(19) $10 + 9 =$

(20) $11 + 9 =$

| 1 | 2 | 3 | 4 | 5 | 6 | 7 | 8 | 9 | 10 | 11 | 12 | 13 | 14 | 15 | 16 | 17 | 18 | 19 | 20 |

■ Add the numbers below.

(1) $2 + 9 =$

(2) $3 + 9 =$

(3) $1 + 9 =$

(4) $4 + 9 =$

(5) $6 + 9 =$

(6) $5 + 9 =$

(7) $7 + 9 =$

(8) $8 + 9 =$

(9) $11 + 9 =$

(10) $10 + 9 =$

(11) $9 + 9 =$

(12) $3 + 9 =$

(13) $4 + 9 =$

(14) $6 + 9 =$

(15) $5 + 9 =$

(16) $7 + 9 =$

(17) $9 + 9 =$

(18) $8 + 9 =$

(19) $10 + 9 =$

(20) $11 + 9 =$

| 1 | 2 | 3 | 4 | 5 | 6 | 7 | 8 | 9 | 10 | 11 | 12 | 13 | 14 | 15 | 16 | 17 | 18 | 19 | 20 |

Adding 9

1+9 to 11+9

Name

Date

■ Add the numbers below.

(1) 7 + 9 =

(2) 5 + 9 =

(3) 8 + 9 =

(4) 4 + 9 =

(5) 3 + 9 =

(6) 6 + 9 =

(7) 9 + 9 =

(8) 1 + 9 =

(9) 2 + 9 =

(10) 10 + 9 =

(11) 11 + 9 =

(12) 5 + 9 =

(13) 7 + 9 =

(14) 9 + 9 =

(15) 1 + 9 =

(16) 8 + 9 =

(17) 11 + 9 =

(18) 2 + 9 =

(19) 10 + 9 =

(20) 6 + 9 =

| 1 | 2 | 3 | 4 | 5 | 6 | 7 | 8 | 9 | 10 | 11 | 12 | 13 | 14 | 15 | 16 | 17 | 18 | 19 | 20 |

■ Add the numbers below.

(1) $1 + 9 =$

(2) $5 + 9 =$

(3) $3 + 9 =$

(4) $6 + 9 =$

(5) $8 + 9 =$

(6) $9 + 9 =$

(7) $4 + 9 =$

(8) $11 + 9 =$

(9) $7 + 9 =$

(10) $2 + 9 =$

(11) $10 + 9 =$

(12) $4 + 9 =$

(13) $3 + 9 =$

(14) $11 + 9 =$

(15) $8 + 9 =$

(16) $1 + 9 =$

(17) $7 + 9 =$

(18) $2 + 9 =$

(19) $10 + 9 =$

(20) $9 + 9 =$

| 1 | 2 | 3 | 4 | 5 | 6 | 7 | 8 | 9 | 10 | 11 | 12 | 13 | 14 | 15 | 16 | 17 | 18 | 19 | 20 |

34 Review
Adding 7, 8, and 9

Name

Date

To parents
Starting with this page, your child will review addition that includes the numbers 7, 8, and 9. If he or she is having difficulty, please encourage him or her to return to the previous stages.

■ Add the numbers below.

(1) $1 + 7 =$

(2) $2 + 7 =$

(3) $3 + 7 =$

(4) $4 + 7 =$

(5) $5 + 7 =$

(6) $6 + 7 =$

(7) $1 + 8 =$

(8) $2 + 8 =$

(9) $3 + 8 =$

(10) $4 + 8 =$

(11) $5 + 8 =$

(12) $6 + 8 =$

(13) $7 + 8 =$

(14) $1 + 9 =$

(15) $2 + 9 =$

(16) $3 + 9 =$

(17) $4 + 9 =$

(18) $5 + 9 =$

(19) $6 + 9 =$

(20) $7 + 9 =$

■ Add the numbers below.

(1) $7 + 7 =$

(2) $7 + 8 =$

(3) $5 + 9 =$

(4) $8 + 7 =$

(5) $8 + 8 =$

(6) $6 + 9 =$

(7) $9 + 7 =$

(8) $9 + 8 =$

(9) $7 + 9 =$

(10) $10 + 7 =$

(11) $10 + 8 =$

(12) $8 + 9 =$

(13) $11 + 7 =$

(14) $11 + 8 =$

(15) $9 + 9 =$

(16) $12 + 7 =$

(17) $12 + 8 =$

(18) $10 + 9 =$

(19) $13 + 7 =$

(20) $11 + 9 =$

Name

Date

■ Add the numbers below.

(1) $1 + 7 =$

(2) $1 + 8 =$

(3) $1 + 9 =$

(4) $3 + 7 =$

(5) $4 + 8 =$

(6) $2 + 9 =$

(7) $5 + 7 =$

(8) $5 + 8 =$

(9) $3 + 9 =$

(10) $8 + 7 =$

(11) $6 + 8 =$

(12) $4 + 9 =$

(13) $9 + 7 =$

(14) $9 + 8 =$

(15) $7 + 9 =$

(16) $10 + 7 =$

(17) $11 + 8 =$

(18) $11 + 9 =$

(19) $13 + 7 =$

(20) $12 + 8 =$

■ Add the numbers below.

(1) $6 + 7 =$

(2) $7 + 7 =$

(3) $5 + 9 =$

(4) $3 + 9 =$

(5) $3 + 8 =$

(6) $2 + 7 =$

(7) $9 + 9 =$

(8) $7 + 8 =$

(9) $10 + 8 =$

(10) $11 + 7 =$

(11) $8 + 9 =$

(12) $2 + 8 =$

(13) $6 + 9 =$

(14) $4 + 7 =$

(15) $12 + 8 =$

(16) $12 + 7 =$

(17) $10 + 9 =$

(18) $2 + 9 =$

(19) $5 + 8 =$

(20) $8 + 8 =$

36 Review
Adding 7, 8, and 9

Name

Date

■ Add the numbers below.

(1) $1 + 7 =$

(2) $3 + 8 =$

(3) $4 + 9 =$

(4) $9 + 7 =$

(5) $6 + 8 =$

(6) $8 + 9 =$

(7) $10 + 9 =$

(8) $2 + 7 =$

(9) $4 + 8 =$

(10) $8 + 7 =$

(11) $9 + 9 =$

(12) $8 + 8 =$

(13) $10 + 8 =$

(14) $11 + 7 =$

(15) $7 + 9 =$

(16) $11 + 8 =$

(17) $5 + 7 =$

(18) $1 + 9 =$

(19) $10 + 7 =$

(20) $11 + 9 =$

■ Add the numbers below.

(1) $2 + 9 =$

(2) $6 + 9 =$

(3) $12 + 8 =$

(4) $7 + 8 =$

(5) $9 + 8 =$

(6) $3 + 7 =$

(7) $3 + 9 =$

(8) $7 + 7 =$

(9) $5 + 8 =$

(10) $4 + 7 =$

(11) $8 + 9 =$

(12) $9 + 7 =$

(13) $2 + 8 =$

(14) $10 + 9 =$

(15) $5 + 9 =$

(16) $6 + 7 =$

(17) $13 + 7 =$

(18) $1 + 8 =$

(19) $11 + 7 =$

(20) $8 + 8 =$

37 Review
Adding 6 to 9

Name

Date

To parents
Starting with this page, your child will review addition that includes the numbers 6, 7, 8, and 9. If he or she is having difficulty, please encourage him or her to return to the previous stages.

■ Add the numbers below.

(1) $3 + 6 =$

(2) $1 + 7 =$

(3) $2 + 8 =$

(4) $4 + 9 =$

(5) $7 + 6 =$

(6) $10 + 6 =$

(7) $3 + 7 =$

(8) $7 + 8 =$

(9) $5 + 7 =$

(10) $6 + 9 =$

(11) $3 + 8 =$

(12) $8 + 9 =$

(13) $11 + 6 =$

(14) $9 + 8 =$

(15) $9 + 7 =$

(16) $10 + 9 =$

(17) $12 + 8 =$

(18) $12 + 7 =$

(19) $11 + 9 =$

(20) $13 + 6 =$

■ Add the numbers below.

(1) $1 + 9 =$

(2) $4 + 7 =$

(3) $2 + 8 =$

(4) $8 + 6 =$

(5) $1 + 6 =$

(6) $4 + 8 =$

(7) $7 + 7 =$

(8) $4 + 6 =$

(9) $7 + 9 =$

(10) $5 + 9 =$

(11) $11 + 7 =$

(12) $12 + 6 =$

(13) $4 + 9 =$

(14) $9 + 8 =$

(15) $6 + 8 =$

(16) $8 + 7 =$

(17) $10 + 7 =$

(18) $9 + 9 =$

(19) $10 + 8 =$

(20) $14 + 6 =$

Review

Adding 6 to 9

Name

Date

■ Add the numbers below.

(1) $1 + 8 =$

(2) $9 + 8 =$

(3) $6 + 9 =$

(4) $11 + 6 =$

(5) $3 + 6 =$

(6) $7 + 9 =$

(7) $2 + 7 =$

(8) $5 + 7 =$

(9) $3 + 9 =$

(10) $5 + 6 =$

(11) $11 + 7 =$

(12) $5 + 8 =$

(13) $6 + 7 =$

(14) $11 + 9 =$

(15) $3 + 7 =$

(16) $14 + 6 =$

(17) $4 + 8 =$

(18) $9 + 9 =$

(19) $2 + 6 =$

(20) $11 + 8 =$

■ Add the numbers below.

(1) $10 + 7 =$

(2) $9 + 6 =$

(3) $13 + 7 =$

(4) $11 + 9 =$

(5) $5 + 9 =$

(6) $10 + 8 =$

(7) $6 + 6 =$

(8) $2 + 7 =$

(9) $1 + 9 =$

(10) $1 + 8 =$

(11) $11 + 8 =$

(12) $8 + 9 =$

(13) $2 + 9 =$

(14) $12 + 7 =$

(15) $10 + 6 =$

(16) $5 + 7 =$

(17) $3 + 8 =$

(18) $8 + 8 =$

(19) $13 + 6 =$

(20) $1 + 6 =$

39 Review
Adding 1 to 9

Name

Date

To parents
Starting with this page, your child will review addition that includes numbers from 1 through 9. If he or she is having difficulty, please encourage him or her to return to the previous stages. If your child can solve these problems easily, it means he or she has mastered how to add a single-digit number to a whole number. Please offer lots of praise.

■ Add the numbers below.

(1) $11 + 1 =$

(2) $8 + 2 =$

(3) $4 + 3 =$

(4) $11 + 4 =$

(5) $8 + 5 =$

(6) $2 + 6 =$

(7) $7 + 7 =$

(8) $6 + 8 =$

(9) $9 + 9 =$

(10) $14 + 3 =$

(11) $8 + 4 =$

(12) $12 + 5 =$

(13) $19 + 1 =$

(14) $20 + 2 =$

(15) $12 + 3 =$

(16) $5 + 6 =$

(17) $9 + 8 =$

(18) $4 + 9 =$

(19) $5 + 7 =$

(20) $8 + 6 =$

■ Add the numbers below.

(1)　　6 + 6 =

(2)　　4 + 8 =

(3)　　7 + 3 =

(4)　15 + 5 =

(5)　　6 + 7 =

(6)　18 + 2 =

(7)　　2 + 9 =

(8)　　7 + 4 =

(9)　23 + 1 =

(10)　24 + 2 =

(11)　14 + 4 =

(12)　　8 + 7 =

(13)　12 + 8 =

(14)　16 + 3 =

(15)　12 + 6 =

(16)　　9 + 1 =

(17)　13 + 7 =

(18)　　7 + 5 =

(19)　　9 + 2 =

(20)　　8 + 9 =

Name	
Date	

■ Add the numbers below.

(1) $15 + 3 =$

(2) $13 + 4 =$

(3) $9 + 6 =$

(4) $3 + 8 =$

(5) $7 + 9 =$

(6) $15 + 2 =$

(7) $8 + 8 =$

(8) $4 + 7 =$

(9) $6 + 5 =$

(10) $1 + 9 =$

(11) $29 + 1 =$

(12) $7 + 8 =$

(13) $6 + 4 =$

(14) $10 + 5 =$

(15) $4 + 6 =$

(16) $10 + 1 =$

(17) $9 + 7 =$

(18) $4 + 2 =$

(19) $16 + 4 =$

(20) $9 + 3 =$

■ Add the numbers below.

(1)　$2 + 8 =$

(2)　$14 + 6 =$

(3)　$8 + 5 =$

(4)　$3 + 3 =$

(5)　$10 + 9 =$

(6)　$27 + 1 =$

(7)　$8 + 7 =$

(8)　$14 + 2 =$

(9)　$3 + 9 =$

(10)　$15 + 4 =$

(11)　$9 + 5 =$

(12)　$19 + 2 =$

(13)　$6 + 9 =$

(14)　$13 + 3 =$

(15)　$5 + 5 =$

(16)　$3 + 7 =$

(17)　$5 + 8 =$

(18)　$9 + 4 =$

(19)　$7 + 6 =$

(20)　$16 + 1 =$

KUM☺N

Certificate of Achievement

is hereby congratulated on completing

My Book of Addition

Presented on _____ , 20___

_____
Parent or Guardian

$3 + 9 = 12$